Publishing history

First Edition January 2013
Email: jediaustin@hotmail.co.uk

Edited by Lisa Warburton

www.isisstockport.co.uk

ISBN 978-1-291-30664-4

Contents

Authors Introduction

A massive thanks for buying this book, it means so much to me. One because you're reading it and I wrote it for you. Two, because I have this mad dream; that if I became famous and rich through my work, I want to help others achieve their dreams. Through putting money into community centres so they can help others achieve their dreams. Whether they are artists, poets, writers, musicians, cooks or whatever, I'd love to put in the money to help.

I'm not interested in the 10 bedroom mansion or Rolls Royce, I want to earn big money so it can help others and that helps me; that's wealth!

Look I'm not condemning those who seek wealth and fortune in titles and a big house, posh cars and whatever, no way. I want the fame and fortune if I'm lucky enough, because it might be and yes would be, the tool to help others, who in turn with their success help others. It's a community dream for me, if I can be an influence to inspire others, WOW! Please God bring it on.

I'd love to turn up at a school in Wythenshawe or a local community centre and give some time and much needed money to help, so that's why I want to be rich and famous. Not for ego, but for how such influence can be used to open doors for others, that would be my wealth.

This latest book of poems is a mixed bag; some of it may be dark but enlightening and inspiring. As a poet you've got to explore all subjects, the bright, the dark, the good, the bad, the cold and uninviting, the warm and the enlightening.

It's lovely to write about beautiful meadows and love, but I won't ignore the dark sad times, like homelessness, prostitution, drug addicts, politics, what and such like, being unemployed and lonely, I will write about it! Not to depress, but only to record an observation, that's life!

So maybe this book is a bit darker than my others but a poet needs to say, "Look here's what I think about the painful side of things!"

This book isn't a negative journal of events; it's a record of certain journey's a soul goes through. The message is this, "No matter what you experience in your physical life, it's only a story, it's not who you really are!"

You're more, we're more than this drama of the flesh, I'm a simple guy from Wythenshawe writing poetry from the heart and soul, I'm just trying to say; "Please, please realise it's all about helping others in pain, not about greed and selfish gain."

Years ago, poets and painters were rich and had wealthy backgrounds, they had the luxury of time to create and muse. Now it's different, the poor artist does exist and that of the writer also, but the wealth is in the work, not the rewards, I love the gift I have been given, to write that is much wealth.

As a writer I want to be a baton that can be passed on to others to take it further, yes I knocked down that obstacle to let you get through. That's what it's about, you never want it to get worse, you want it to always get better.

I welcome fame and fortune, so I can have the money, influence and tools to help make it better.

Question

As a poet, do you think poetry is dead?

Answer

No never, people do it in text or on the phone, or in the coffee shop, as well as other places. Poetry to me is an expression of the soul, a reflection of one's own thoughts, so poetry will always be alive, as long as people are alive. It's the exploration of emotions whatever the media is, the baring of how it feels and thinks to be a human, that's poetry. The spoken word of an expression is poetry, even if you don't write a poem or think you're a poet. To me it doesn't matter, your expression as a person of anything, I believe is a kind of poetry.

The moment you have an opinion or thought about anything, that's poetry.

These poems in my latest book are my view point on life, that's all. I'm not saying it's right or wrong, but for me, if anyone says I don't believe that shit I will write my own poetry; that's a great success. If people think 'I like that', then of course I say thank you, but if it inspires, that's everything.

I Love Wythenshawe

Verse One

I love Wythenshawe because it's a great place
to me,
I've heard some say it's horrible, but I'll never
agree.

The memories I've enjoyed and discovered
there,

I couldn't have found and lived in any other
where.

Wythenshawe Park for instance is a beautiful
place,

Its makeup always paints a smile on my face.

Verse Two

I love Wythenshawe, oh yes I do,

It's given me a lot so I'd like to say thank you.

Lots of great friends and special memories I've known,

That's why dear Wythenshawe lives in my hearts home.

Yes there's been laughter, fun, sorrow and tears,

But those are the seasons of growth that bring fruits to the years.

Verse Three

I love Wythenshawe because it's in my blood,

Yes the so called bad times and the good.

It's like a stage I've lived a life upon,

I always miss it when I've left and gone.

Most of the time the skies above are grey,

But the playgrounds of Wythenshawe have always brightened my day.

Verse Four

I love Wythenshawe and I'll never forget,

All of its treasures I've discovered and met.

Like climbing trees, jumping across streams and scoring a goal,

It's just a part of my jigsaw that makes the picture whole.

I've been lucky to meet some of life's greatest people here,

Their kindness and generosity has been so precious and dear.

Verse Five

I love Wythenshawe because it's been good to me,

When I arrived from Ardwick slums it was a lovely sight to see.

That was 1968 when I was only eight years old,

Wythenshawe was Manchester's garden city of nature's gift of gold.

Verse Six

I love Wythenshawe because I have seen,

How rough and bad other places have been.

I think its people have great humour and wit,

There's a great wisdom that says 'make the best of it'.

So my appreciation and respect is true,

When I say with an honest heart Wythenshawe I love you!

When the sun sets down

Verse One

Every time I see your face,

The sun comes shining through.

All the thought I have,

Is all because of you.

I see you smiling at me,

It really makes my day.

I wish you were by my side,

But I know you'll always stay.

Every time you're smiling,

There's no face wears a frown.

You're always there to comfort me,

When the sun when the sun sets down.

Chorus

In the colours of a rainbow sky,

I see you everywhere.

In the colours of a rainbow sky,

You left your love to share.

In the colours of a rainbow sky,

In the colours of the sky.

Verse Two

Memories of your life,

Help us through each day.

All those dreams of you,

Bring another chance to play.

When the tears of sadness fall,

You always cheer us on.

In the heavens of our hearts,

You've never really gone.

Every time you're smiling,

There's no face wears a frown.

You're always there to comfort me,

When the sun, when the sun sets down.

Chorus

In the colours of a rainbow sky,

I see you everywhere.

In the colours of a rainbow sky,

You left your love to share.

In the colours of a rainbow sky,

In the colours of the sky.

I'll be Right by Your Side

Verse One

There's one thing you have to know,

In this world where we all grow.

Through the good times and the bad,

Those happy days and the sad.

When you're feeling on your own,

You don't have to be alone.

Chorus

Coz I'll be right by your side, yeah, yeah yeah.

My love for you won't hide, yeah yeah, yeah.

Coz forever you will see, yeah, yeah, yeah

How much you mean to me, yeah, yeah, yeah.

Verse Two

There's one thing I'd like to say,

Love yourself in every way.

All you'll ever need to do,

Just believe in being you.

Through the good times and the bad,

Those happy days and the sad.

When you're feeling on your own,

You don't have to be alone.

Chorus

Coz I'll be right by your side, yeah, yeah yeah.

My love for you won't hide, yeah yeah, yeah.

Coz forever you will see, yeah, yeah, yeah

How much you mean to me, yeah, yeah, yeah.

The Spirit Smiles

We are not the roles we act and play,

The vesselled pot doesn't make the clay.

A shadow is not the parent of sunlight,

But only its child in day and night.

The wooden chair that's born out of a tree,

Is no longer a nest for birds to fly out free.

If greatness is based on medals and attributes,

We might as well say feet are made out of boots.

You know what I mean; we've forgotten who we are,

If we believe that the driver is worth less than the car.

All that is buried and considered dead,

Is the stories that we've created from our own head.

The flowing waters don't sing I'm just a river,

As it turns once again to the mouth of its giver.

In the moment you hang a label upon your soul,

You suffer in that attachment of its impermanent role.

It's a powerful life the one you are creating,

They'll always be thin ice that needs breaking.

No telescopes can move the stars any nearer,

All they do is magnify their face a little bit clearer.

The flower knows every petal lost as it fell,

But it didn't refuse to bloom and say life is hell.

We are not the roles we act and play,

The spirit smiles inside the bodies decay.

Never Born to Die

Verse One

I was never born to die it was just another
dream,

Remember that wise saying; things are never
what they seem.

I didn't come to vanish in the funeral of deaths
pain,

My spirit keeps on dancing in transformation
once again.

I never died to be born that was just another
dream,

I'm not in times yesterday or future because
I've always been.

Forever is eternal and it's only our concepts that
have an end,

The law of attraction always brings what your
strongest thoughts send.

Where is here and where is there does anybody
know?

When it disappears in every moment did it ever
go?

Verse Two

If god is in the mirror of everything we see,

Are what we call reflections second hand
shadows of what used to be?

If you want to find heaven then you must have
been in hell,

If you want to ride the biggest wave you've
known a smaller swell.

When I go to bed and fall asleep I know I'm
somewhere real.

Every world I've experienced,

My heart and soul can feel.

I was never born to die,

It was just another dream.

I'm not in yesterday or the future because I've always been.

The Mystery of Reality

What is this world we call reality?

It's beyond my knowing and conceptuality.

In the madness of it all where's the sanity?

I can't find it in the senses of physicality,

Could it be something in the mystery of spirituality?

Are laws of karma to do with past mortality?

Every single thing on Earth has duality.

Is the dreamers dream their own normality?

What do you think is your reality?

Take a Second Look

Verse One

The prison of life's delusions makes a slave out of you and me,

When we hold on to the surreal it drowns beneath the atomic sea.

Trying to capture one fleeting moment in the flowing river of now,

Would be like thinking you could milk a calf before it becomes a cow.

To learn something different and new about ourselves each day,

Would crack the egg shell of wisdom.

Open and release our weary way,

The name that we name is not the true name.

This Earth play you're in,

Is just a changing game.

Verse Two

Perhaps the art of being beautiful is to just be you,

Maybe the reflections and mirrors are showing what's not true.

Did you ever stop your circus parade and take a second look,

To realise you have wrote every page of your life's story book.

How the villains and the heroes of your dramas flourish and decay,

As the curtain of every scene closes and opens night and day.

What is the ego's greatest crime but to bring loss and pain?

As in its separation from others its kingdom is special again.

Awareness is the souls golden treasure that tells no lie,

God gave wings to the caterpillar, so death could not kill the butterfly.

Running Scared

Verse One

The hunters are coming to murder a life away,

Riding through fields and meadows to enter the fray.

The blood hounds are chasing an innocent smell,

To catch a poor creature in the teeth of their hell.

The fox flees the devil disguised as a man,

Running in fear as fast as it can.

But the distance is closing until there is none,

As the killers have spotted the unlucky one.

Verse Two

Blowing their horns to signal attack,

The souls of the riders fall off their back.

Wearing a smile as deaths on its way,

The hunters sing loudly to champion a slay.

Their hounds from hell frighten the air,

As teeth bite in to strip bones bare.

Surrounding to kill and tear it apart,

They fight each other to rip out its heart.

Verse Three

Its cheers of delight and drinks all around,

As the hunters celebrate the death on the ground.

The screams of the fox sing its last song,

But that's music to the ears who hear no wrong.

In this shadow of darkness there's no hunters tears,

Because they don't know the victims fears.

Verse Four

They call it sport and entertainment for fun,

But they'd soon be scared if the fox had a gun.

While evils around the hunter will say,

It's all a part of natures culling anyway.

Somewhere in a fox hole its family must grieve,

You can call me mad but it's what I believe.

So running scared is all sport and fine,

Unless it's your life of course on the line.

When the Rain Poured Down

Verse One

I remember when the rain poured down it
made the buildings shiver,

As the windows of my wet house, were crying
like a river.

I saw the water bubble and boil as it raced
down the gutters and grid,

The greasy puddles on the pavements seemed
to laugh as people slid.

Now welly boots and rain macs,

Were blooming like flowers in their prime.

As I heard in the news,

Blackpool's sandy beaches had turned into mud
and slime.

Verse Two

When the rain poured down it lasted for a
week,

We must have had half a dozen buckets in our
house for every leak.

Outside hiding heads found shelter under the
mushroom of an umbrella,

But as a kid, I loved the waterfall that fell down
our coal cellar.

As the rain bounced on pavements making a
splashing crown,

The petals of flowers drank it up before they
drown.

When the rain poured like a sea,

Some cursed it like a crime,

Wishing it could do good and fall on a desert
clime.

The Power of Gratitude

Verse One

The power of gratitude is a wonderful thing,

Appreciation is the best song to sing.

Count the blessings in your life,

There's more of them than pain and strife.

Those happy things that make you smile,

Walk with them daily in every mile.

When you feel what you are grateful for,

Its magic wants to deliver more.

Verse Two

Even when the fog of sadness clouds your eyes,

There's a new sun for you just about to rise.

It's hard I know when you can't see hope,

But let me tell you there's a way to cope.

It's the power of gratitude I'm talking about,

So here's my mantra I'm going to shout.

If it inspires you to compose your own,

Like Dorothy in the Wizard of Oz, you'll return back home.

Verse Three

I'm so grateful for the birds that sing,

Such pretty music to my ears they bring.

A colourful flower sharing its fragrant scent,

The friendship of a person in this precious time spent.

The gift of being you to this lovely planet Earth,

The power of gratitude appreciates your worth.

If Dickens was Alive

Verse One

I'm living in the estate of a council slum,

Where if you aint got a job you're called a bum.

The politicians promise if you vote my friend,

We'll bring you all injustice and suffering to an end.

It's just another lie, coz we've heard it all before,

Just look how the government treats injured soldiers after war.

The Queen comes out from a palace and says, "I understand",

But if you knock on her door for water, then you'll be damned.

Verse Two

The unemployed hang about on corners with no
place to go,

Ducking and diving as they try to make their
prospects grow.

Mrs Murrays ugly but her daughter looks so
nice,

"You gotta marry a rich man", is her best advice.

The neighbours peep behind their curtains with
a sneaky eye,

That's the closest they'll get to the theatre
before they die.

If Charles Dickens was alive he'd have another
book,

Nothing's changed since his time except the
way things might look.

Verse Three

Where's the friendly police man walking down your street?

Wasting time on Facebook and Twitter on a tweet.

Feeling like a failure as you sign on the rock and roll,

You weren't born on this planet to be a slave to the dole.

No prince can ever understand when you can't get a job,

A drink and a weed is a dummy to the tears you sob.

A care taker in a brothel would suite me fine,

At least I'd be guaranteed lots of over time.

Verse Four

The wisdom I learned came from the streets I walk,

You can tell a bull shitter by the patter they talk.

The prisons are full of stories that you wouldn't believe,

Unless you wore their shoes,

Sinner cast the stone and leave.

Did you see a preacher put a penny in the plate?

Or a government that didn't condemn those poor souls on welfare state.

If Charles Dickens was alive he'd have another book,

Nothing's changed since his time except the way we look.

Homeless feelings

Verse One

On a cold dark night I was scared and alone,

Living on unpredictable streets without a home.

My comforts are cardboard, blankets and a newspaper pillow,

As I beg in the day my proud head hangs like a weeping willow.

Please could you spare some change for a cup of tea,

It's hard to ask when you see the eyes that look at me.

It gets me down but at least I'm still alive,

I'm as cold as a bee in winter that's lost its cosy hive.

Verse Two

I've got old clothes on my tired back and
moneys hard to get,

The dirt that covers my fingers stops my hands
feeling cold and wet.

When I was born my parents couldn't cope or
care,

I'd only get in the way of their selfish addictions
if I was there.

So please don't judge me because it could have
been you,

I'm glad it wasn't, but remember a homeless
person has feelings too.

Verse Three

Yes I dream of a job and a family to love and
adore,

That would be true wealth in my life that's poor.

I know it could be worse, like living in India with no shirt,

Even looking to eat worms in the putrid soils of African dirt.

There for the grace of God go I so spare a coin if you can,

Because if you do it's never wasted by a homeless woman or man.

I'm so glad this poem can express a different point of view,

So if you can spare a coin, then God bless you.

Your Spirit Knows

Verse One

The streets are freezing over in a frozen age of cold crime,

We'll all be living in an ice age if we don't chill out in time.

Everybody has a skeleton that's shocking to the bone,

If you're cheating in a sordid affair, you're bound to feel alone.

Every hidden corner offers a bunker to peep and stare,

But once you blink and look away it might not be still there.

Making daisy chains in the summer grass,

Skating on thick ponds of winter's hard face of icy glass.

Verse Two

When we get a smell of nostalgias shadows of
yesterday,

Who could be blamed for being fooled into
bringing it today?

When we try to kiss a moment that our lips
can't hold,

For one taste wouldn't we give a whole world of
gold?

Teenage heroes you pinned on your bedroom
wall,

Fall into decay and oblivion as each birthday
came to call.

When a second of your life comes and goes,

That's entertainment that only your spirit
knows.

It's a Part of You

Spare a thought,

As you piss your life away.

There's always something good in a shit load of waste I say.

Nothing ever disappears,

It just keeps on going around again.

Turning into food for the soil and water for the rain,

So spare a thought and I swear this is true.

Somewhere out there, that pretty flower and tree,

Is a part of you.

By Boz 2

Question

What's this poem about Ged?

Answer

Everybody's life really, in fact, every living things life on this beautiful planet we call Earth. So what we call waste makes the next life and what we call life makes the next waste and soon it's obvious to all, it goes on and on, that great eternal unbroken circle, you can call God, if you want.

Question

Why did you sign it Boz 2 instead of Ged Austin?

Answer

It's my tribute to Charles Dickens. Fans of his books will know who the Boz one was, so I thought I would sign it Boz Two.

Embrace Life with a Kiss

Verse One

I woke up this fantastic morning feeling happy
and fine,

Hey being a poet of words is like a spider
spinning its line.

That's what we both have to do and I don't
mean maybe,

I like to see the growth of innocence that
started as a baby.

Verse Two

Everywhere I throw my look it's just all energy
and frequency of vibration,

What's that mysterious dance of eternal source
behind all of creation?

Yes I'm talking and thinking about this and that,

It's the house of soul where nothing's really ever at.

Verse Three

How glad is that centre of peace that lives inside a storm?

Can you feel the pulse of inspiration fuelling avant-gardes new dreams born?

The poet is stone dead if those inner eyes go blind,

Every conceptual artist dabs their brushes with psychic colours from the mind.

Verse Four

No camera ever lets you see the eyeball of its voyeuristic host,

We could be more dead than we know from the viewpoint of a ghost.

As a lens catches a fleeting moment of light that
takes just a blink to miss,

The message wrote in the D.N.A of every atom
is embrace life with a kiss.

Window Shopping

Verse One

I was looking through a window as I saw you in a shop,

Appearing rather elegant your beauty made me stop.

I thought your eyes had trapped mine that day I saw your face,

While deep inside my beating heart my blood began to race.

Great tidal waves of happiness shivered my shaking bones,

Fires of burning passion lit up my erogenous zones.

Yet all we seem to do is stare the time away,

The births of words from your mouth are not part of this play.

Verse Three

I'm just another passer bye that's fallen in your trap,

You love admiring compliments and an audience to clap.

Instead of giving me your love you turn away and shun,

All I ever wanted was a friendship built on fun.

Goodbye sweet girl I murmur it's time that I should leave,

Things are meant to be, that's what I believe.

So as I turn to leave this window shop in space,

Another foolish dreamer arrives to take my place.

A Great Cup of Tea

Verse One

Now I'm not an astronomer that can observe
the path of planets and stars,

Now I'm not even a Blacksmith that can forge
molten metal into strong iron bars.

Now I'm not a brave soldier that can go to war
and win a medal,

Now I'm not a champion racing driver whose
foot presses hard on the accelerators pedal.

Now I'm not even a trawler fisherman that
braves the sea for cod,

Now I'm not even a Preacher speaking a sermon
from God.

But here's what I know I can do,

Make a great cup of tea to bring pleasure to
you.

Verse Two

Now I'm not a genius professor that can invent
a clever thing,

Now I'm not a champion boxer that stays
undefeated in the ring.

Now I'm not a mountain climber that can scale
Everest's top,

Now I'm not a deep sea diver that sinks to the
bottoms drop.

Now I'm not a professional footballer whose
name the crowd call,

Now I'm not a pop star hanging on a fans wall.

But here's what I know I can do,

Make a great cup of tea to bring pleasure to
you.

U.F.O

Out there,

Out there,

U.F.O.

Take me with you,

I want to go.

Far away from this pain and grief,

Now that would be a sweet relief.

Out there,

Out there,

U.F.O.

Take me to a better show,

Far away from this lonely crowd.

To a place of peace,

Where the noise aint loud.

Out there,

Out there,

U.F.O.

Let me tell you what I know,

There's more to life than meets the eye,

So let me see your different sky.

What is Art?

What is art but an abstraction taken out of
natures mine,

Yes, the appearance of shadows creates the
illusion of sunshine.

Removing the dream out of the dream to save it
for another sleep,

Is like taking the salt out of tears before those
emotional rivers weep.

X-ray eyes that search below the surface and
see the great atomic dance,

As the forms of illusions that we took for
granted surrender their solid stance.

Photographing moments in an iceberg that
never freezes the image away,

But it's just ancient sunlight caught on a film we
call yesterday.

Vibrations and signals travel through space and the air that we breathe,

Landing on the planet of somebody's brain as reactions and responses leave.

What is art but a feeling of creation?

Whether it's appreciated or not.

You may call a rose beautiful or ugly,

But it's still got what it's got.

The Daily Drama

In the daily drama between night and day,

One always seems to be eating the other away.

As the Earth's blue stone spins and revolves,

Around a golden sun that pulsates and evolves.

In the daily drama between atoms and cells,

Unfolding stories reveal creations heavens and hells.

As its universe hides wonders and secrets beyond eyes,

Breaking down the old so the new dreams can rise.

In the daily drama between thoughts and mind,

Clouds of happiness and sorrow to find.

Building illusions and spinning fates thread,

All your life was a world in a head.

Learn to Love Yourself

Everybody's future comes from the here and now,

Like a farmer gathering crops,

First we have to plough.

The past is a ghostly echo that left its voice to die,

We can never live yesterday under a flickering lighthouse sky.

The present can't be stopped in the physical human being,

Death is the driver that takes us to a place that's unseen.

This world of vibration is a frequency to be explored,

But if you learn to love yourself,

Then an inner peace is assured.

No one Wins a War

Verse One

When that deadly missile left its nest to swallow up the air,

The name of its poor victims was not its thing to care.

Above the ground that blossomed with trees and flowers sweet,

Blazed and burned a devil with blood and tears to meet.

Born and made to explode flesh and bones into a splatter,

Generals decorate themselves because war victims don't matter.

Verse Two

Military hardware profits think peacetime is so bad,

Looking for another conflict makes money out of sad.

Homing on its target to rip human guts apart,

Don't expect a moral inside a weapons heart.

Born to kill the living of those in its way,

The missile is a monster that ruins a family's day.

Curse the fool that ever brought this thing to Earth,

If you thought that Judas was the worst.

Then what's that person worth as missiles may hurt flesh and bone,

But the soul it will never reach,

No one wins a war isn't this what death does teach.

It Shines to be Seen

Verse One

The lonely weed blooms sunshine as its fragrant
scent released falls unloved by humans amongst
chosen heads of favourite flowers,

In heavy wet skies above grey clouds billow
towards their bursting grave of death that
deliver life giving showers.

The four leaf clover promises the seeker of it
rewards of good fortune as it hides in the
meadows of a grassy green sea,

Shimmering twinkling starlight dances through
the universe peeping out and appearing from
curtains that are part of eternity's mystery.

Verse Two

The thoughts born in every mind that offers a
cradle for it to be like a stone radiating through
the still waters of a pond,

Oh how those butterfly wings softly flapped can create vibrations of heavens or hells far beyond.

So always remember what shines to be seen even if gone unnoticed has far reaching powers,

Never forget the lonely weed that is harshly judged unfavourable,

By some is loved as one of God's beautiful flowers.

We are Blind

Verse One

What eyes do you really see with?

Not the ones that make illusions live.

When showering judgements on fleeting things,

Can you hear the whispers that falsehood sings?

As you cast thoughts and anchor on
disappearing shadows,

It's like planting seeds on a million barren
meadows.

No truths were ever captured by the physical
eye,

Think how often your own vision of it has been
a lie.

Verse Two

When we drink water from an emotional sea,

How often does it poison the senses of you and me?

In the gap and space of that slowed down wink,

Is found a timeless meditation of nowhere for thoughts to think.

In the angels perception of sight we are blind,

The needle in a haystack is a moral we can't find.

The Fashion of Death

Verse One

In the high street of fashion there's a murder to
be found,

Draped across some back where death doesn't
make a sound.

People wearing fur coats with the guts all
scrapped away,

Where rivers of blood used to flow night and
day,

Now long since dried away into the soil and the
dust.

All to satisfy someone who's a slave to the
desire of fashions lust.

Where's the bones that held it firm I think we all
should know?

Where's the heart that used to beat to make
this creature grow?

Draped across the hunters back; it's how it all
began,

The kingdom of the animals is under threat by
man.

Verse Two

It doesn't matter to the crowd that never hear
the screams,

Vanity covers the conscious like closed eyes
kept in dreams.

Cat walk models sell their souls to wear the
latest kill,

That's the death of fashion making money at
the till.

Stripping all the flesh away as traders cut a
profit,

Madam try this fur coat on it's such a perfect fit.

Where's the bones that held it firm I think we all should know?

Where's the heart that used to beat to make this creature grow?

Draped across the hunters back it's how it all began,

The kingdom of the animals is under threat by man.

Verse Three

On the high street of fashion a haunting sight goes by,

Displaying all its bloody charms without a tear to cry.

Where's the bones that held it firm I think we all should know?

Where's the heart that used to beat to make this creature grow?

Draped across the hunters back it's how it all began,

The kingdom of the animals is under threat by man.

Nazca Lines of Peru

Verse One

Strange unexplained lines in Nazca carved in the floors of deserts in Peru,

Could these be runways for spaceships for ancient astronauts to land on too?

Mathematical designs of geometric animal mysteries only seen from above the air.

Because if you walk and view them from the ground you can't see the formations there.

Could it be possible these were markers to guide aliens into land?

Are we that foolish to dismiss such a theory out of hand?

From worlds so far away where distances are vast,

Could we have been visited and influenced by super-intelligences from the past?

Arriving from different stars on a mission to Earth,

Might they have discovered man and helped improve his worth?

Verse Three

Did they plant seeds of cosmic knowledge in primitive earth-heads where none had been before?

Was this the missing link that searching anthropologists would discover and been blown away for sure?

You can imagine human-beings being transfixed and bowing in worship like only they could.

Worshipping these space gods that gave us some of their D.N.A. code and blood

Verse Four

Imagine what fantastic powers they soon revealed to stun both woman and man,

As they left us with maps of the galaxies and the meanings of life's wonderful plan.

Maybe from distant stars of tiny pins of light millions of light years away,

They reached a point of their history when war and ecological disasters ended their planets day.

Verse Five

Could they have been survivors on a ship we recall as Noah's Ark but the sea was space?

Then they eventually came to land on a beautiful blue world we know as Earths face.

A home of giant beasts called dinosaurs that had to go,

If this was to be a world to begin again and grow.

Verse Six

Look, I'm not saying it was or wasn't but if you keep a closed mind,

There's never going to be a door of a different discovery to find.

Could not a comet of been directed to end these prehistoric creatures reign?

So life from other worlds could start here again.

Verse Seven

The pyramids and other structures have still never been explained,

The history books in schools are full of lies and to the mind of reason are pained.

So what did happen many thousands or even millions of years ago?

Maybe, the honest answer is, from this position in our time, we'll never know.

Verse Eight

From my own point of view and for what it's worth,

Do I believe super intelligences from other planets have visited this Earth?

"Yes", without a doubt and I will always know this to be true,

As for the Nazca lines, I believe they carved them in Peru.

Question

Why is this book called 'I love Wythenshawe'?

Answer

Well, it's a place I've grown up in and loved and learned much from, met the most amazing people in, had my first girlfriend, played for my first football team and had lots of my first experiences of different kinds of things; too numerous to mention.

Most of the headlines I've seen about Wythenshawe have been about its crime and dark places, so I wanted to give it a headline albeit in my book which glorifies and praises the great things about Wythenshawe which has much more good than bad in it.

So that's why my latest poetry book from one of its sons is called 'I Love Wythenshawe'.

Question

It is a first though isn't it Ged, someone praising Wythenshawe?

Answer

Maybe, perhaps it is but if it is then it's long overdue. Yes, I grant you that so called pop stars or actors or whoever has got a nice slice of the honey of fame and money does say, "Oh it was a rough, tough, hard place Wythenshawe" and all that contrived shit to make them look better but those idiots are lying and they know it, they are trying to make out they are working class heroes, but they are not. I'm saying what is right on, Wythenshawe rocks; it's a great place to live.

Question

Is this book a tribute to Wythenshawe?

Answer

Well in as much as it is one of its sons, me, Ged Austin being a poet and a writer born out of that special place and saying 'I couldn't have wrote the books I have if I hadn't lived and breathed its air, so yes in that way it's a tribute.

Question

What's so special about Wythenshawe?

Answer

Well first of all, it's people, they are so cool, funny, kind, loving, down to earth, that's why I will always love Wythenshawe, yeah of course you get scum, you'll find that anywhere, Hale Barns, Wilmslow, where ever, but Wythenshawe has got great people in it.

Questions

So called pop stars, actors or whatever, who leave Wythenshawe and never return to it or put anything back into it, what do you think about them?

Answers

They are all shits who have forgotten where they came from and without Wythenshawe they wouldn't be where they are now, they might be materially richer, but in terms of the spirit they are poor.

Look if I do or when I do coz, I like to be positive, become famous, I really would enjoy helping out this place and its community centres, like I've mentioned and schools, how cool would that be? Fantastic I think!

There's a lot of great brilliant talent in Wythenshawe; it's a gold mine of lovely people I'd like to help.

Question

This is your 14th published book to date, what keeps you writing?

Answer

My imagination I think, but the fact, not that I might make a million pounds out of it, but the buzz a million people might get some pleasure out of reading my stuff and if someone is inspired to write it better, wow, that's even cooler I think.

I don't write to be right or wrong I write because I love it. That's why I'm rich really, because I love it!

Question

Finally can you give any advice to other writers?

Answer

Yes, write it as you would talk it, don't copy any style, just be you. Yeah, you'll be influenced by this writer or that, but never think I'm not good enough because they write better. No I say, what you've got to say is important.

Look Charles Dickens, Mark Twain, C.S Lewis, Lewis Carroll and many more, they would wipe the floor with me in terms of writing, but what I've got to say is different. So as a writer honour that difference because if it touches one heart, it's always been worth it.

Printed in Great Britain
by Amazon